# *Time's Web*

Look to see no end
And no beginning,
But Time, the immortal spider,
The orb-weaver,
Forever spinning.

# Time's Web

*Poems by*

## *Ruth Moore*

*William Morrow & Company, Inc., New York  1972*

*For Eleanor Mayo*

# Contents

# Time's Web

# The Ghost of Phebe Bunker

Here by the flung water,
The ice-cold, gray-green glitter in cloudy sunshine,
On a beach of tossed pebbles and jingle shells,
Huddles their lost town.

Against the sky some roofless, windowless houses,
An alder-grown curved road climbing a hill,
A wilderness wilder than it started out to be.

This is the place they came to.
This is an island
A mile-and-a-half across and three miles round.
In 1766, it was black to the shores with spruces.
Indians came there in summer; by the south beach they left
    abandoned
Some burnt-out firepits; stone circles where the wigwams were;
A shell mound.

Who has seen it recalls a place of sweetness, clean smells,
    pure sound;
Spruce needles warm in the sun; bayberry bushes;
Salt from the wind; the soft, slow, airy cradle-swing of
    water moving;
White-throated sparrows and the hermit thrush.

After the journey, after the long running
Through fog and sunshine, east on the southwest wind,
Coasting it down,
They found this harbor, safe for little ships,
Some shallow ponds, with marshgrass for the cattle.

Less than two hundred years was their time here,
Theirs and their sons,
Who now are names on stones.
O Grandfathers,
Atlantis under the sea is not more drowned in water
Than your dead town under its sea of spruces.
Your faces are in the lintels of these doors,
Your fingerbones wrought into the granite of this hill.
After so many sailings, settings out,
This is where you landed; after all.


The sea rolls cream and froth, gray-green, ice-cold,
Wind blows through empty parlors, rotten with rain,
Saying, they came, they lived here, they died.
They changed nothing?
No loss? No gain?


The curled weed dried among the pebbles
Is here, as when they came.
They did not change the dead sea urchin in the goose grass,
He is the same.


Only,
They left some adze marks in the rotten timbers,
Squared a few stones to make a cellar wall,
With bulkhead doors to open, saying, "Harvest, come in."
Saying it now to the ant with his aphid,
The fieldmouse with his seed,
To moonlight and witchgrass and the yellow weed
Whose roots are where the footprints were.
"Harvest, come in,
Be here under the tough stones that long ago
Flung in the teeth of the murderous, black northeasters,
A barrel of apples, a potato bin."

*II*

My name is Fair Andy
I lead a black life,
I'll steal all your money,
Make off with your wife.
And when the bright morning
Puts out its cold star,
I'm away to the Indies
And islands afar.
        So
        Sweet ladies, remember
        Me body so brown,
        And the nights with Fair Andy
        You spent on the town.

Accordion and organ on this hill?
Fiddle notes where the granite foundation sinks in the turf,
And over it the goldenrod grows high?
This is a cricket; this is the southwest wind,
Blowing up the hill through the weather-scraped lintels of
    the lost town.

Still,
The great man gravely writing $E = MC^2$
Wrote also that no sound is ever lost.
Follow the waves of it into time, he said,
Fast enough,
Far enough,
There will be Waterloo, the Sermon on the Mount.

So, equally there, might be old Freeman's voice
Singing "Fair Andy" while the dance goes round,
Spin-your-partner, grand-right-and-left!
Odd man out yelling, "Tucker!"

The *thunk* of the dropped broomhandle hitting the floor,
Scuff of his shoes as he grabs him a girl,
Dance beginning again;
Albert's accordion, Will's fiddle, old Freeman's
    nose-stopped-up tenor,
May's organ, the woosh-wheeze of the bellows,
Thump-thump of her little feet, firmly pumping.

These sounds were lost on the wind so long ago:
May's name and Albert's, Freeman's and Will's,
Death's head and weeping willow, are lichen on slate,
The organ silent, the sweet singers gone.
Yet on this hill,
Where indestructible sharp seeds
Hurry, hurry, hurry
To put back a wilderness gone a hundred years ago,
A man can turn his face southwesterly
So that the wind lies over his ear like a seashell,
And hear,
Far off and not a tune, oh, not "Fair Andy,"
No note so deep as an organ-tone, so high as the skreek of a
    fiddle,
But a sound, surely; a lost, unquiet music,
As if the cosmic gales that snatch away
The clang of time and wars, great words remembered,
The voice of the man himself saying $E = MC^2$,
Had from their roaring flanks let fall some small and
    unregarded notes,
Which, filtered by terrible void, drift, homesick, back
Into the orbits of familiar stars,
Into the southwest wind, the soft, warm wind,
That blew them from this hill so long ago.

### III

Phebe Bunker
Left Heaven early,

Sneaking out through the pearly gates when Peter's back was
   turned.
They in Heaven didn't like you to leave there.
Peter had told and told her.
"Phebe, you stay put! Or I'll have to tell God and He will
   tend to you."
But Phebe couldn't help it.
From the top crystal tower of the great gold wall,
The one Lucifer fell from (or so They said),
She could look off through a trillion miles of stars
And see, like the lost blue stone from someone's ring,
The little earth. And so she had to go.

If They in Heaven want us to forget it,
She told herself,
They better not leave it around where we can see it.
It wasn't my choice to trade what I had there for choir singing.

Light as dust, down through the stars and planets,
Falling,
She thought about Heaven. Some thoughts, perhaps, that
   wouldn't be quite manners
To think while you were in there. After all,
The place had been set up by a batch of real good old men,
But tired. They must have been, to want to rest forever.
You had to face it, there was a sameness to Heaven that
   sometimes got to be tiresome.
The worst mistake They made was not to let in animals.
Cats and dogs would have helped out; Phebe missed a cat.
On earth she'd always said she couldn't keep house without one.
Another thing, this quarter of Eternity belonged to the
   Baptists,
And you were out of luck if you didn't like Baptist hymns.
Then there were all those people,
The ones you weren't exactly glad to see dead and buried,
You only thought, at last you were rid of them for good.

Abel, Frank, Joshua;
Isaac, Maynard, John;
Uncle Lew, Aunt Diana; their kids, the cousins;
And more coming; on and on and on and on and on.
Every last one of them sitting in Heaven,
And this time, no end to it. This was forever.
Made you wonder sometimes, Where's Hell? Or if there was
    one.
Well, that was what they wanted.
Heavenly Rest was what they asked God for,
And what they got.
Anything they asked for, they got,
Like now, the Lost Atlantis.

That's all laid out, nice as you please, in another part of
    Heaven,
For those ones that things on earth never went to suit.
All kinds of cronies, Abe Lincoln and Tom Paine,
My seventh-generation grandson Joel, and that old Greek with
    the long whiskers I never can remember the name of,
And many more too numerous to mention
Asked for the Lost Atlantis, and got it.
But do you think any of them spend any time there?
I heard the whole works of them carrying on, complaining,
Because folks at home were still squabbling over colored
    people,
A hundred years after the Emancipation Proclamation.
A colored gentleman named Mr. W. E. B. Du Bois carried in
    word,
And came out and told what God said, and He was right:
"That if He'd known beforehand making people of different
    colors was going to create such an uproar, He'd never have
    bothered.
All He was after, anyway, was a little interesting variety."

He's strange, God is.

He isn't a nice old long-whiskered grandfather,
That's for certain.
He's a Spirit, and you never know what a Spirit will do.
So I will think these thoughts now,
Never in Heaven.

Falling, light as milkweed-down, drifting,
Falling for long and longer,
She went and went and went and went and went.
Didn't seem to be getting anywhere, though she knew she was.
She'd done this before, but she had to realize now
It was a far piece, since They moved Heaven.

That was a thing, it surely was, that day,
When They in Heaven had to move in a hurry,
Because the sounds of some great monstrous heathen battle
Gone roaring round through time century after century,
Doing just what the man said such things might do,
At last caught up with Heaven.
Oh, that was a day, indeed!

There they all were,
Pearly gates, pavements of blue and jasper,
Ivory towers,
Everyone cozied in.
Harps tinkling,
Choir singing.
A lady named Daisy MacHazy had hit high C and was
    holding it,
To the astonishment and miration of all the angels,
When over the wall and down the peaceful streets
Came belting in a horrible, hollow booming,
Crashes and hubbubs, screeches and clangs and whacks
That shook the towers of Heaven and even rang a bell or two.

Some knew it for what it was, remembering

The last sounds on earth before the arrow or the spear thrust
    or the club had smashed them down;
But anyone could tell it was a helmonious great fight
    somewhere,
With people being murdered and saying so.

Cherubim and seraphim scattered in all directions.
Wing feathers flew. It took all afternoon to sweep up the
    feathers.
Phebe recalled how she had swept and mended.
They always called on her to sweep and mend.
(Those were things she did well, she swept and mended.
She liked to; it helped to pass the time.)
She trimmed a loose pinion and tacked it back on the wing of
    an old Greek angel,
Who shook and shook and turned as cold as ice,
Kept crying, "Marathon, Marathon, Marathon!"
And couldn't be comforted.

So They in Heaven set the whole works in motion,
Whizzled it off through space like a railroad train.
Mercy God, couldn't have that in Heaven!
Heaven was peace, Heaven was promised peace,
For some, that is, for old and tired people,
But not for Phebe Bunker, who looked back
And saw, smaller and farther off, but shining still
The little lost blue stone from someone's ring,
And thought, I'll go;
And went;
And, sometime, got there.

She landed on a hill she didn't know,
Grown with long grass the color of a lion,
And running juniper swept over by the wind.
Shadows stroked along, one after another, of big white
    clouds in a blue sky.

Sakes, she thought, I've lit on the wrong island;
Miscalculated somewhere, though it's not surprising,
There's a little million of islands in this bay.
But then she saw the stones, the old foundation,
The rectangle, sunk in, where bulkhead doors were gone
And lay below, gray-mossed, with field weeds growing in
    them—
Things you'd never know had once been wood,
Unless you knew they were, for sure.

Could this be our house and nothing left of it?
Where it was, hardly a hole in the ground?
You wouldn't think anybody'd ever lived here, had a baby
    or a good time,
Or washed a kitchen floor.

That lilac bush with the tree all pushed up into it
Might be the one I buried Tommy alongside of, I don't know.
The place where he'd be is all grown over now.
Tom? Tom-Tom? Tommy? Are you still there?

He came, thrusting out through whips of lilac,
Stirring the leaves with his big bruiser's head.
He had the one blind milky eye he got in a
    knock-down-drag-out with a gander,
The other like a green malignant grape.
The crook in his tail where Jerdan's dog almost caught up
    with him was there,
And the thunderous loud purr which she remembered,
Scooping him up, nudgeling his head under her chin.
You old devil, you still feel prickly as a burdock.
I always told you that pelt of yours was more like hay than fur.

Well, the last time I came back, I didn't walk up this hill;
Spent my time in the town, looking at houses;
Nobody in them then, but they were houses still.

From there, I could look up here and see the place where we
    used to live,
And from the graveyard gate I could see it standing, plain
    as could be.
Somewhere along, I must have lost track of time.

That's Enoch's hayfield, sure enough, right there.
All his life long he worked his fingers to the bone
Keeping running juniper out of it, and what's it now?
Running juniper.

From here, she couldn't even see the graveyard fence,
Only the wind-swung tops of a forest of spruces.
Trees where the town used to be, and big trees, too,
No house, no rooftop. Trees had swallowed everything.

Tom, in her hands, was clawing to get down.
Well, you ain't changed, she told him, watching him go
Ahead of her, spy-hopping through the grass.
Wild as a wolverine, and never could take but a little mite
    of loving.
Thought the whole world belonged to you, was yours;
For sixteen years, hadn't a reason to change your mind,
Until the day, old fool, you tried to sharpen your claws on
    the stallion's leg.
Look at you now, light as a bird, jumping that grass.
You always were, never felt heavy to lift,
As if you had air, or feathers, under all that rough shag.
Only when I dug the hole by the lilac bush and put you in,
You were heavy then, and so was my heart.

Under her foot, if she pushed hard with her toe,
She could feel the cart-track in the stony earth—
The wheelworn rut that a hundred years of grass had failed
    to fill.
Some of it, ground into granite outcrop, she could see,

Covered with moss, but there
If you knew where to look.

My, the wagonloads Enoch's hauled up this hill!
Barrels of flour, kerosene and sugar,
Molasses . . .
Once, when he went to Boston on the vessel,
He brought back tamarinds as a special treat.
"Tamons," he called them.
Funny-shaped, like little skate's eggs, and sour-tasting.
I never did let on I didn't like them.

I can see the oxen on that frosty morning, breathing white,
And him, proud as a rooster because he'd got home safe
    and brought back everything he went for.
We had our hungry seasons, sure enough,
But after the first years, we managed, and managed decent,
    too.
I never saw the time here I couldn't make a vinegar pie.

She walked on, slowly down.
There was the graveyard fence.
Well, shan't you die! she said, looking in wonder.
Some of them trees are a foot through at the butt, and
    bigger ones fallen.
But that fence ain't down, and it ain't going to be,
No matter how you trees lean to push it over.

That's teak, that fence is, the real old teak from China,
Or wherever it was from, I disremember now.
Cap'n Joe Jerdan brought that deckload of wood back from
    round the Horn,
Planned to build a fence around his premises with it,
To show that he'd made money and at last amounted to
    something.
Seeing, as a boy, he'd never had a pot to catch pea-soup in,

He thought a teak fence would be a well-thought-of thing.
But when he landed home, late March . . . let's see.
Early April . . . sometime in the spring . . .
That was the winter the white throat-disease hit here,
Killed half the young ones, quite a number of the grown.
All of us had it. Some got over it.

Cap'n Joe Jerdan found his house tight shut.
All that was left of his wife was her tulips coming up.
He put his fence around what he said were his premises now,
Left in his vessel and never came back again.
You'll work, you trees, to shove that teak fence down.

"It must be teak," a voice said, quite close by.
"Even cedar would have been down long ago.
Well, it could be teak,
Those old boys all had vessels,
Somewhere to sail to and come back to,
Something they thought worthwhile bringing home.
Teak from the Orient,
They could have lugged it round the Horn."

It gave her quite a turn.
She said, Oh!
And, For the land's sake!
And, Who're you?
To the young man leaning on the fence.

He didn't hear her, but he heard something—
A sound that seemed to blow by on the wind,
Too quickly lost among the tree-boles,
Not voices, nor fiddle sound, nor organ; not accordion,
But something.
Phebe heard it better than he did.

That was "Fair Andy," it surely was, she thought.

Now, wasn't that nice of May and Will and Albert and
    Freeman
To make me feel at home.
This young man doesn't see me or hear me,
After all, I'm just a ghost.
But he got a little something out of them.

He had. He'd turned his head to listen,
But after a while, he shrugged and went on talking.
"Oh, any man with a long nose can split the wind with it
And hear a sound in his ears if he wants to.
Old Homer's men heard the same thing over water and
    called it sirens.
Or woman-sound. They had been too long at sea.
I could call it the past; I have been too long in the present;
The past's distilled music.
If the gone time left some kind of sound, a man might hear it
    in a place like this.

"Well, Grandfather,
Was that your ghost?
Did you have something to say to me,
Or do you want to know how things stand with the country
    now?
If your ghost is anywhere in that mess of rotten bones,
Let it listen.
A little of the news is worth hearing, I guess.
Most of it isn't."

Phebe slipped past him into the graveyard, looking for a
    place to sit,
Seeing familiar names on stones.
There was her own stone, flat as a flounder, in the witchgrass,
Not cracked, but you'd have to poke around to read it.
She didn't need to; she knew what it said.

PHEBE
Beloved Wife of Enoch Bunker
1750–1850
A good woman is her husband's fortune

Well, so I was, she thought. At least, he always said so.
Too bad it's been let to tumble over. It was real pretty
    when 'twas new.
Had a weeping willow on it.

She sat down on the only grave that showed enough of a
    mound to make a seat.
It was Joel Bunker's,
Her seventh-generation grandson, counting four to a century.
He'd been the last man to live in this town, to die and be
    buried here,
A hermit, living alone.
She'd sat here on her last trip down from Heaven.
It had been a new grave then, higher, more comfortable to
    sit on.
She was surprised to see Joel himself already sitting on it,
    smoking his pipe.

You never get away from them, she thought.
And said, aloud, Move over, Joel, will you?
And please blow that filthy smoke the other way,
It smells like a barn burning.

He said, What have you resurrected that old tomcat for?
You can't take him back to Heaven with you, you know that.
Only people go to Heaven. People. With souls.
He hasn't got one.

That makes it nice, she said. Doesn't it?
So people with big, plentiful, fat souls
Don't have to bother with anything underfoot in Heaven.

He grinned and blew his smoke, not caring where it went.
They wouldn't let him in even if you asked, real pretty,
Which I don't believe I've ever heard you do.

No, so you haven't, have you, Phebe said.
I never was one to haggle with God and whimper to him,
"Oh, dear God, I'll be good, if only you'll do so and so."
When I had troubles, I handled them myself,
Not like some, who hermited up on this island,
Cussing the world because God wouldn't fix up what I
    thought was wrong with it,
Sucking my finger while the place went to rack and ruin,
And my own house fell down around my ears.

Weather's the devil, it tumbles down most things
He said, and puffed his pipe. Take your tombstone, there,
All you can tell by that rotten old slab now
Isn't that you lived a hundred years,
But only that you've been gone a lo-oong time, Grandmaw
    Phebe.

That's right, she said, and that was all she said.
She wasn't about to chew any more rag with him,
That is, if she could help it.
She might not be able to help it.

Why don't you just shut up that clack of yours and listen
    to Chris, Joel said.
That's him, Christopher Bunker, on the far side of the fence—
My grandson, nine generations down from you.
He's the modern man;
Once called himself a liberal; perhaps he still does.
I was; my father wasn't; Chris's father wasn't.
It seems to skip generations, somehow—
By that, you can sometimes tell what's coming next.
Chris is the last one of us left on earth.

He's come here for today to see what else is left.

He hasn't found much standing, thanks to you,
Phebe said, under her breath,
Except the graveyard fence.

"We've had one hell of a war since you've been gone,"
    the young man said.
"Only, in our time, we don't say 'war,'
We say, 'The lights are going out all over the world.'
And by God, they did,
And we're still waiting for them to come on again.
We've invented the big bomb, the final one,
So final that any joker who gets his hands on it could blow
    up the world;
So big that every country on the map wants one for Christmas.
We did that. Out of it we got two dead cities.
And we've been to the moon.
Those are the great news items.
I always say, first things first."

My, you've been busy, haven't you? Phebe said.
Why on earth would anyone want to go to the moon?
I've been by the poor thing several times,
And I wouldn't care to land there, let alone think a trip
    to it is any great shakes to brag about.
Or were you looking for somewhere to take your bomb and
    leave it?
From the shape the moon's in, there's likely been one such
    bombilation go off there already,
And another one wouldn't matter much.
I can't think of anything better to do with such a thing.
Let's hear what else you've done.

"So far as I'm concerned, I teach in a high school.
Things go well enough with me.

It's not a bad life.
I get fed up sometimes, the way a man does.
I think to myself if I have to listen to one more slick
    politician,
See one more too-fat teenager sucking on a bottle,
No matter what kind of sticky brew is in it, just so it's a
    bottle,
If one more smart operator says to me buy-and-sell,
And things, things, things, things for the people
While the world goes to hell in a handbasket,
I'll kick in some faces and some picture-tubes,
But all in all I do as well as any.

"At my place on the mainland in the afternoon,
When the shade grows long with the slow gathering-in of
    night,
The little cats come home, tired of hunting,
Happy for fish,
Making peaceful sounds over a saucer of milk.
Yesterday, I dug potatoes, wrote a little, read the morning
    paper,
Wondered if the chrysanthemums would have time to bloom,
Before the cold nights mowed them down;
Tried to see if the shape of the country, standing tall and
    proud in the sun,
Cast a shadow; and what the shadow is.
Grandfather?

"Let's see.
I wonder what you'd most like to hear.
Shell beans are dry in brown and yellow jackets;
Hens are laying again; squashes are ripe.
I grew a big squash this year.
Remember the big squash Henry Thoreau told about growing
    in the corner of his garden
That weighed a hundred and twenty-three pounds and a half?

And how he said, marveling, in a speech before the
  Cattle Growers' Association,
'The seeds were my ferrets,
Which I sent into the earth to hunt it out,
Who would have thought I had a large yellow squash
In the corner of my garden?'

"At night, in my house, the fire is lighted,
The television turned on.
Voice out of the living room crying, 'Love me,'
Over and over, urgently crooning, 'Love me,'
Somebody wants
Somebody else,
Tender and earnest,
Sorrowful, sincere.

"This is September in an election year,
The season of the smear,
The bawling, hoarse and venomous,
The beautiful, the old phrases running off the tongue.
*What did the man do with the dollar?*
*Pay his office help?*
*Buy a house?*
*Go to Florida?*
*The man says, "What dollar?" and goes on with his speech.*

"Oh, Grandfather,
These are the times that try.

"Over the sweet, the too-sweet, the corny singing,
Over the voices calling cheat and traitor and rotten politics,
I listen for the grave and beautiful voice of my country."

The young man stopped and stood for a moment listening.
The wind sang in the trees, whispered in the weeds
Over the quiet places of the dead,

But there had been nothing Phebe could hear,
And Joel sat, serenely
Sucking on his pipe.

"Out of the archives and the histories
What forgotten sound, blown by on the wind,
Of the truths held to be self-evident?
Who says, now?
Jefferson? Whose word creates a flurry on both sides among
   the viewers with alarm?
No, nor Lincoln,
Because we have malice it would seem, and the cause of
   charity is cold;
And shall I tolerate my neighbor or he me
Longer than it takes him to kill me because I have to try
   to stand him?

"Who says?
What words?
We have nothing to fear but fear itself?
Thoreau said that and Roosevelt quoted him,
But not we.
Fear itself is the bogie under the bed now,
And who remembers 1850?
Or 1932, when we were so little afraid?

"What do they say?
      'Throw it out and buy new?
      Why make a thing to last
      When built-in obsolescence
      Is where the money is?'

"Proud shadow of my country, tall in the sun,
Like Lot's wife?
Or a column of snow?
Like a hope for generations to come?

"There in the old and rocky earth,
My squash (twelve pounds) found room to grow.
Its roots went down to find trace elements
Our people might have put there, years ago.
Fall is here,
Crisp, cold.
The leaves ready;
The jeep-track by the garden lined with frost.
Under the trees the shadow of winter sits like a blue ghost;
Another winter in our little time of less than two hundred
   years
Of snug roofs and warm fires,
Of children fed and women comforted,
Sleep in the night and waking in the morning;
Of seeds to dry,
Rivers to run.
Less than two hundred years to say the bones of liars in our
   earth
Do not outweigh the bones of honest men?
Or to cry the thieves' grief down the bloody centuries,
         'Men, brother men, who after us shall live,
         Let not your hearts too hard against us be'?" *

Joel Bunker got up, knocked out his pipe on his tombstone,
Made a moderate sound, something like "Hum-ha,"
And began slowly to fade.

So you are headed back for Abraham's bosom, Joel,
Phebe said. Where you are comfortable and safe.
To say, "Hum-ha" to God and wrangle with Him.
God isn't going to do anything, and you know it.

Well, He ought to, Joel said, out of his mist.

* François Villon, Andrew Lang translation.

God started it, let it go on without lifting a finger.
It's up to Him to finish what He started.

Then what did you come here for?
Why did you come?

From the far side of the fence, the young man's voice
Lay on the air like darkness, as if the day already turned
    toward night.
"What am I here for? Why did I come?
Did I think I could let Grandfather know about the Lost
    Atlantis
He told me we all might build in times to come,
If we set our minds to building on something more than the
    sound of some old bells
Ringing out of the ocean on a stormy day?
'Trash growth,' he said, 'comes first and then the spruces.
You don't need to cut everything down to give the trees a
    chance to grow.'
*Don't you?*
Grandfather?"

And I'll be merrily surprised if that isn't just what you're
    going to do, Phebe said.
Cut it down, let it go to rack and ruin, blow it up,
Have yourself one hell of another fine war.
Judging from what's left after all your fights and hubbubs,
    so far,
You think that's all you *can* do.

What are you so rumped up about war for? Joel said.
(He was nearly vanished now; his voice came out of the cloud
    of his own tobacco smoke,
As if he had lit his pipe again, for the journey back.)
War is one of the symptoms of being human.

When in the world didn't we have wars,
Again and again and again?

Yes, whenever didn't we? Phebe said.
My father and my brothers, all three of them,
Died just as dead from musket-balls in '76
As anyone could die from this great splendid bomb he's
    told about,
And I don't doubt there were some of the same old dirty atoms
In the tomahawk of an Indian.
Oh, pu on fools!

You're all the fools of the world and always have been.
You could have fixed things up two thousand years ago,
There was a nice chance for it then, and any fool can argue
    out a difference.
But no; you've had to fight it out.
Century after century, and you've still got to be prancing
    around fighting.
This one's got something someone else wants;
That one's got a grudge.
Someone's a different color, or thinks different.
Doesn't matter,
Just so you get an excuse for blood to flow.
Thing is, you like to fight.
Gives you a chance to boss each other round,
Belong to something that moves you all the same way,
On the same foot,
In the same clothes,
At the same time.
I'd think after all the centuries you've had
Of wars and getting over wars, and seeing what they do,
    first-hand,
You'd figure out a way to get along.
You give me, if you want to know, a pain in a funny place.

So go on back to Abraham's bosom and cuddle,
It's the best place for you. The only place, if you ask me.

You're a tiresome old woman, Phebe, Joel said.
Your nosy pudd'n stick is into everything.
They in Heaven told you to quit bothering us in Atlantis, and
  you did.
Told you not to come back to earth, and here you are.
Who do you think you are—somebody's conscience, or
  something?
I've got an in with Peter, let me tell you,
And when I get back there, I might just persuade him to
  slam the gate.
You know where you'll go and your tomcat and your
  broomstick with you,
If They won't let you back into Heaven.

He faded, this time for good, but his voice came back thin
  and shrill out of the cloud he vanished into,
Better get going, old girl.
You're not so young as you used to be,
And it's a far piece up through the stars and planets.

So it's a far piece, is it? she said, mimicking him.
Let it be known it isn't the first time I've traveled a far piece.
I traveled one to get here.
I sailed oceans, three thousand miles to get here.
Five hundred more, up a stormy coast, to get here.
So what's a trip to Heaven?
It's not Heaven I'm homesick for, you big-mouth!

"Homesick," Chris Bunker said, from the far side of the fence.
"Homesick, homesick, homesick,
The weed for its wilderness,
Man for his greatness,

Who is not without defense against the dead coon full of
    12-gauge double-ought buckshot
Flung on the town dump;
Who, beside the deer's gutted carcass swung from the tree
    in the wet November air,
Sets out a bird-feeder."


Yes, and you, too, my ninth-great-grandson, Phebe said,
Carrying that face of yours like a doubled-up fist.
I'd like to take you and your father and all the rest of them,
Abel, Frank, Joshua,
Isaac, Maynard, John,
And stand them alongside of me on the deck of that dirty little
    coaster,
The morning twenty of us saw this island come up out of the
    morning fog,
With the sun slanting down on it, milky on the spruces,
And the clean, green water, where it curled into white
    on the beaches.
I'd like you to see what we saw, that day, after what we had
    come from.
Filthy, we were; stinking.
My dress, when I took it off at last, took with it some of the
    crust that was my skin.
I was sixteen; Enoch and I had just buried our first baby.
In the ocean; naked, in the ocean.
All we had was what we stood up in.
I would have torn a piece of my dress,
But Enoch said it was decenter to let him go the way he was.


I heard you say, a while ago, that children are fat now.
"Too-fat teenagers," was what you said.
You've had a bait of them.
I'd had a bait of too-thin ones, including me.
I was twelve years old when I saw a boy hung for stealing
    a piece of bread.

So there you are, crying for Lost Atlantis.
I tell you we saw Atlantis that morning, rising from the sea,
Dressed in green trees and cleanness,
And hope for children to come.
It was not Lost Atlantis, it was found that day,
And with no sound of rusty old bells ringing,
But birdsong from the shore and white gulls crying over the
     harbor.
If it's lost now, it's you and your likes who lost it.

I tell you, I have seen the streets of Heaven,
Great, shining towers, all anyone thinks it might be,
And Heaven is pretty, there you can rest in peace,
If peace is what you want.
But I would trade Eternity now for what I saw that morning,
That new beginning, that chance that came once in a lifetime,
And will not come again in anybody's lifetime,
Unless it's made to come.
If I could be here, and young again, and find the children
     not hungry,
I wouldn't spend my time crying gloom and disaster over
     an old graveyard fence.

# Time to Go—1930

In the afternoon, the sea turned thunderous green,
Clouds massed in the west.
Near islands stood out big and clear; distant ones, through
    some trick of the air,
Lifted their ends out of water, as if the tide had tunneled
    under them.
The man said, "The land looms."
He was trip-lining a skiff,
His anchor fell with a *chunk* into the still water off the beach.
"What makes it?" I asked. "Is it the thunderstorm coming?"
In a way to say that the look of things was sometimes too much,
He shook his head.
"Sign of a storm or a cold snap, in the winter. Been long,
    since I seen it in the summertime."

He took his pipe out of his pocket, looking sideways at the
    clouds,
The sky was the color of an old black eye; far out, where the
    mirage of the islands loomed, growing surf was soapsuds
    white.
It seemed detached from the rest of the sea, which flowed
    under it.

Beachrocks rattled under his boots as he sat down.
"I seen them islands loom in wintertime like they was cut in
    two in the low places on'm.
Of a gray morning, cold, I seen them islands look like
    double-ender dories."

The spruces would hummock together, weighed down with
    snow.
Except for his threshold, his tracks, no other footprints,
No boat but his, upended on the beach,
No fish-house but his opened and the banked crust scraped
    away.
Of a gray morning, cold, the ice would grind in the harbor,
The islands would loom, the islands would be
Double-ender dories in a bleak sea.

"Time and again," he said, "I seen this cove so black with
    seabirds
You couldn't see the ice for'm.
On this beach, of early morning, cold, I seen seven million
    tracks,
Where the sea ducks spent the night.
They heap up the snow in front of their breast, and it kind
    of melts round'm,
Leaves a little cradle, like."

I said, not thinking, "You must have time on your hands,
To sit and count so many seabird tracks in winter."

The look on his face was not so much disdain as nothing.
I could see his face close itself against me.
These things were true, serious to him.
Sorry, I tried again. "It's lonesome here, in winter?"

He said, "Likely we'll git a tempest pretty soon.
Thought I heard thunder rumbling, didn't you?"
I had been hearing it for upwards of ten minutes, but I
    didn't say so.

"I hate a goddam thunderstorm," he said.
"Runs in our family, I guess.

I got a relative goes in the closet, shuts the door and rolls his
    head in a raincoat."

In the west, a streak of lightning split the clouds
To the top of a mainland mountain, which at once
Began to vanish in a haze of rain.
"Look at that damn thing," he said. "Hear it sizzle, if your
    ears was good enough."

He knocked out his pipe, and with the air of a man who's made
    his mind up, gave me a straight look.
"There's people all around here in the summer.
They come and they go."
His look said, And you're one of them.
You come and you go.
He didn't say this, only made it clear,
And then went on.
"I'm here the year round. I got critters to look after."

He waved his arm at a field, where two plain cows,
One red, one white-and-red, were tied to graze.
"Them and a horse—he ain't worth much now—
Four pigs, two cats, a dog, forty-three hens
And seven pairs of doves.
I had some mallards, once, for about ten minutes,
I sent for them from a game farm,
But when they come, I opened the crate and they flew off.
I ain't seen them since.
They're around here, though. They're somewhere in the woods
    and ponds.
I know they must be here.
So I ain't moving away. If they ever come out, I want to be
    around to see'm.
That drake was as handsome a bird as I ever laid eyes on.
If you'll excuse me, I'll put them cows in the barn.
I never had one lightning-struck, but they might be."

He got to his feet, started, turned around.
"I thought both them cows and that horse was struck by
    lightning.
Once, I thought they was.
I found all three of'm laying by the cattle spring,
Flat on their backs, taps-up, feet in the air.
Lightning, I thought. Couldn't be nothing but lightning,
Except there hadn't been no thunderstorm I was aware of.
I was all set to skin'm, sharpening up a knife,
When, by God, they all begun to come to.
So I never skun'm.
Good thing I didn't.
I've often thought it was."

He went and led the cows in, unsnapping the stake ropes,
    dropping them where they were,
And came back walking between, with a hand on either halter,
Like an old brown Greek priest with his beasts, only these
    gentle and not for sacrifice.
I heard him talking to them, something without words, or
    no words I could hear,
And was startled when they answered something without
    words;
Or maybe it was only the green grass rumble in their stomachs.

He braced the barn door closed with a stick and came back
    sidelong,
Looking up at the sky with much the same glance which he
    had given me.
"Now that I've gone to the trouble to put them cows in the
    tie-up before it's time,
Likely that tornado'll pass off to the south'ard of us.
Hell, that's the way it is.
There's always something."

"What was it?" I asked.

He looked again at the sky; came back and sat down before
   he answered.
"What was what?"
"You walked off before the end of the story."
"Oh, them cows, you mean. And the horse.
Well, it got to be a mystery-to-God before I figured out what
   ailed'm.
In a couple of hours, they was wandering around the pasture.
They wasn't happy at all, but they was living.
I see the horse aim at a tuft of grass
And land chewing a thistle eight inches to one side of it.
And I see one of the cows yaw round and walk on her ankles,
Just to the world like old John T. Sebasticook,
An Injun, used to come here after sweetgrass to make
   baskets of,
And had a squaw brewed the strongest dandelion wine I ever
   tasted.
And all of a sudden it come to me.

"A spell ago, when them damn dry women forbid the use of
   liquor,
We had a rumrunner come ashore here on them ledges yonder
   and break up in an easterly.
I got me about ten cases of nice French brandy out of her
   before she stove up entirely,
And I stuck it all in a little cave, like, back of the cattle spring.
That's the spring, over there, under that tall rock.
Freezes sometimes, when the weather's cold enough.
I seen ice come down that rock like a yeller curtain.
I don't try to water no stock to it, in winter.
But it was April when them cows and that horse come, as you
   might say, to grief there.

"So I went out and tasted, and sure enough, it was.
Frost coming out had bulged up the rock, made a little cave-in.
One, or maybe, two, of them cases of brandy was squat flat.

What that spring was running was the nicest kind of a mix of
  brandy and water.
Lasted about two days. Them cows and the horse and I
Had us a high old time. None of us ever forgot it.
My wife (she was alive then) couldn't fathom it.
Why on earth would a man go and drink out of a cattle spring
  when we had the best well in the county?
Nasty, she said, drink after animals.
Oh, well, she's good and gone a long time now, poor thing.
She was death-and-jesus on any kind of alcohol.

"I bottled some of that whilst the mix was running.
It's nice.
You want a taste of it?"

I had some, while the storm passed off to the south'ard.
The black bruise left the sky blue and the sun came out
  while we sat there, having the taste.
It was good French brandy, potent, not mixed with anything
  so far as I could tell.

He watched me drink.
"Well, time to go," he said.
"I'll let them cows out now. That horse is dead.
Fell down, a long time ago, rooting at the ice out in that spring.
I had to shoot him.
Come again.
Good-by."

## Ballet for a Typewriter—1932

Rat tat, woodpecker, knocking on a wall,
Earn your living though the heavens fall;
Tea, butter and a cinnamon bun,
Eat it and like it, little one.
Pay your cash in essential ways,
You can have steak on the holidays.

Trees that the weather has gone over three hundred years,
The Great Watering Place where he took his cows to drink,
The sloop he went swordfishing in, the *Bonny Belle*,
Orion and the moon over the Methodist steeple—
Whatever made my grandfather a good man,
He died believing he was.

Methodist, Baptist,
And Puritan they lie,
Without an ounce of proper flesh
A man might know them by.
Roofed by Creation
Blanketed with sod,
Each expects presently
To rise and go to God.
With a foot on the mountains
And one in the sea,
Stout Angel Gabriel
Will blow lustily,
And strong earth juices,
Rain and shining sun,

Will start working backwards
To clothe each skeleton.

I was the woman in the taxicab,
Being taken to hear *Traviata* at the Hippodrome.
There were evergreen trees on the sidewalks because it was
    Christmas,
And over them,
Drifting down,
Fine snow.

In 1913,
When we cut the Christmas tree in the Alder Swamp,
Through the sweep of the plumed woods, far off, with dignity,
A sound of water over ledges echoed,
Receded,
And was still.

Window full of colored balls,
Window full of ostrich feathers,
Window full of blue glass Christmas trees,
Traffic whistle by,
El, roar south,
Lights of Sixth Avenue,
Muffle and drown in snow.

All the little devils
Down in hell,
Tapped with their hooves
On the sulphur stones;
*Bling!* says the devil,
*Bling!* says the bell,
Rattle up the old man,
Rattle up his bones.
They are dancing down in hell

To a noisy castanet,
Shaken in the fiery gloom,
Shaken in the heat.
They will give you bread and tea
And keep you from the wet.
Fling away those feathers, gal,
You have got to eat.
You will get up in the morning
You will go down the stair
To the bare, swept courtyard,
The alarm clock's bell
Buzzing in your ears the
Taste of coffee in the air;
That sound is not the sea, my dear,
That is just the El.

On Brooklyn Heights
It gets dark early in December.
The East River goes past the foot of Montague Street
The white Bermuda liner looks like a wedding cake,
She is going into sunshine and a blue landfall
Tomorrow.
The *Berengaria* means business
No coastwise, Gulf-Stream trip for her.
By tomorrow she will have left even the gulls behind.
The gray breast of Mother Sea for the *Berengaria*.
O whistle of the white Bermuda liner,
Whistle of the *Berengaria*
Whistle of the tugboat going under the bridge!
Outside the room on Thirty-second Street,
Each day the tree of heaven spilled its leaves
Until there were no longer any leaves to fall.

Grandfather, Grandfather,
Put aside your quilt
Of spruce and red granite,

And spend the day with me.
Here's a dry martini left,
(Some of it is spilt)
Here's a snow-white ostrich plume
To trim the Christmas tree.
Grandfather, Grandfather,
God is in the sky,
He will take you home to him
Every scattered bone.
He's a putter-offer,
He'll come by and by,
In vast poetic whiskers,
Something like your own.

In August the small blue flower whose roots were in the
    beachrocks,
Began to remember winter, the roll of the wave, the salt spray's
    sting.
The sandpiper ate snails, nodded to his reflection in the
    tidepool,
Cried out,
And then took wing.
The fog at sunrise whitened over the harbor,
The water was very still.
He heard the whisper of his boots in the fog-wet witchgrass,
And the ripple of the bore along the beach.
Your dory was full of fog, my grandfather,
Your herring-weir was full of silver fish.

These are dice
In a square black box,
*Bling!* says devil,
*Click!* say dice.
Sit in your chair while
The woodpecker knocks,
And think your thoughts

Which are not quite nice.
In a seablue peacoat
Buttoned and trim,
And snow on his shoulders
Think of him,
From sin and weather
Lying hid,
In a juniper root
And a coffin lid.

I am that woman, knowing Christmas was coming soon,
Who could have looked upon Orion and the moon,
But said, "Draw closer to me, for this old
Intolerable reticence is very cold.
I know it is late. I know. It is very late.
He was a good man, but he is dead.
He would turn in his grave, no doubt, if thought of me
Could penetrate the clay above his head.
But beauty is in your most remarkable face,
And this will be my Christmas gift to you,
Riding this cab along Sixth Avenue,
Between the evergreens, between the streetlamps' drowsy glow,
With your fingers touching my fingers for a space,
And on the cornices of the buildings, snow."

# On Celebrating Christmas Eve—1933

I say it is cold outside for a human skin.
A rabbit's pelt, fur on an otter's throat
Would not keep out that wind. See, on my coat
How eagerly it drove small snowflakes in.

I came down on the Elevated; I
Arrive in sadness; must apologize
To you, your fire, and your Christmas rye.
Perhaps it was some singing in the steel
As we came south by whitened windowsills,
That made me think of wire stretched and strung
And humming over country-pasture hills.
(A very lonesome sound, you will recall.)

Or, like enough, it is the sight of all
My good friends here, with light upon their faces
From this small, blue, sophisticated tree;
Or sundry beers I had in various places.
And beer, at best's, a melancholy thing.

I've come in feeling like a plucked heartstring.

Let us be gay. It is the Holy Night.
The Wise Men now tot up their holy dough.
The blessed giver asks with lovingkindness
If Santa please will bring a radio.

Over in Jersey now, in Westchester,
The patron saint of all sits on the lawn,

Gay in his colored lights; and how he winks
Through the blown snow, and flashes off and on.

On Beacon Hill, it is the carol singers,
In overshoes and furs, with bells, and tight
As billygoats from hell, who gather cheerily,
Under the lamps, begin on *Silent Night*.

The Charles is like a silvered block of ice,
Stabbed with faint light; the Common is a glow
Of stormy bulbs; the trains swing eastward and the rails
Hum like taut wires over country snow.
(A lonesome sound, my friends.) The carol singers
"God rest you" to the wind, and harmonize;
Behind them lies New England, with her coast
Drowned in appalling seas, and like a ghost,
With the gray blizzard driving on her from the skies.

My friends, it is a stormy night. A ring
Of bacchanalian revel fills the air.
I came in like a sheet of paper and a piece of string
Off a Christmas package. I am not going anywhere.

But tonight I will stay here and be gay with you,
In the blue light of this incredible tree.
I shall watch your faces grow hazy and unprotected,
Blurred where the shadow falls, and mine will, too.

And then, in the gray morning, at six o'clock, I think,
I will get up and leave you and go away.
Over Manhattan, over the windows, it will soon be day,
Across Manhattan, the snowplows will be beginning
To tear apart the purity of the snow;
Filth will be falling on it in the thinning
Darkness. My friends, we are young, we have been elated,
And full of the Christmas spirit; I shall go
Home, as I came to see you, on the Elevated.

# The Mountain of Snow—1934

As when a little snow, tumbled about
Will make a mountain.
W. Shakespeare

## I

New England, in my blood and in my bone,
Recall to me my flinty heritage—
Daisy and everlasting, saxifrage,
The slow, reluctant blooming out of stone.
Tough land, recall my toughness of a knot
In hickory wood; the root the boulder bent;
For I unlearn the stubborn words you taught:
Whose breast the sea strokes lies indifferent.
Recall the icy eyes of gull and gannet,
Wingbones and devil's aprons, eels and caves,
For, oh, my fathers in their capes of granite
Are turning, turning, turning in their graves,
That I should be so tamed, caught unawares,
Pliant and passionate. A child of theirs!

## II

I do not think, my dear, that spring returning
With wild wet winds to blow its blooms away,
Ever again will set the blind blood burning,
As once it did, in springs before today.
Not spring nor fall, nor any changing season,
Nor petal blown, nor river in its flood,

Nor Beauty's self could be sufficient reason
For this upsurging clamor of the blood.

Therefore, be gentle with me; love me never
So much as now, who in your hands have laid
All lovely things to keep for me forever,
That all the springtimes of my years have made;
Perilously keeping for myself alone
The fearful flame, consuming flesh and bone.

### III

This is not new; it is only new to you.
The strength within it soon will make it old.
The human syndrome, steeled in dust, foretold,
Needs only flesh to show what it can do.
See how it flowers there along the nerve,
The candelabra-branching ice and fire,
Path of a lover's fingers, in desire
And tenderness, to trace a body's curve.

No. It was older than primeval cloud,
When the first tiger sprang, the first wound bled;
Therefore, be not ashamed nor over-proud
That ancient custom cradles you to bed,
Heavy as time, strong as a lover's kiss;
But not in tenderness nor love; not this.

### IV

I think you do not love me; but be kind
Awhile tonight, and do not tell me so.
Let me stay here and watch the firelight find
The dark foam of your hair before I go.
So quietly the shadows touch your hands,

So frail a spell the falling embers weave.
This is a silence that one understands
How not to break, but dare not quite believe.

Oh, I perceive how all the pitiful rest
Of love is dead and done with; but the strong
Dark tentacle of beauty in my breast
Irrevocably curled, must last as long
As I shall live to keep a small, sublime
Deluded ghost from creeping out of time.

## V

The rocks will never miss you, nor the sky.
The sea will be unchanging, oh, my dear;
Tomorrow by this water, only I
Of all things else shall know you are not here.
There to the sea tomorrow's boats will go,
Tomorrow's petrel cut his windy track
Across the cloud-rim; only I shall know
That you are gone and are not coming back.
Somewhere in time, remote beyond belief,
Compassionate summer leased to you and me
A sheaf of days as beautiful and brief
As bubbles, rising, breaking, in the sea.
Remember them for me and help me bear
Pitiless water and impassive air.

## VI

The small brown birds are going now; the oak
Lets down his leaves, and frosty fields are bare.
The days of summer, they were less than smoke,
Less than a flight of sparrows in the air.
Light as the bird's wing, softer than her breast,

First snow, for ground the ice has rent apart;
O lovely snow, fill up the ruined nest.
You cannot heal disaster in my heart.

Oh, flake by flake, creep up the bending bough,
And cradle deep the melancholy leaf;
No one but I remembers summer now,
Scattered in time and lost beyond belief.
Kindness on stone, on seed and stubble row,
But not upon my heart, O lovely snow.

### VII

Wherefore was I by you a changeling made,
Who tore me helpless out of flesh and bone,
And in my heart as in a cradle laid
A creature unfamiliar and unknown?
That was not I, tormented by a face,
Beset, by fear beat back, and wholly sad;
For I was one who loved you with the grace
That long ago a sunny childhood had.

See now: his wings are scattered to the north,
His body flung asunder in the west;
Your child become a goblin, going forth,
Leaves fierce and bloody claw-marks on the breast
That harbored him for enemy or friend.
Wherefore was this? To what ungentle end?

### VIII

Wake not to life, O dreamer, for your eyes
See now the compass-point where quest is ending;
Love is a falling star across your skies,
You touch no hand, you do not need befriending.
By this, your dream, you are remote and far,

Wake not from sleep, you do behold the dream;
Forgotten be this life, this falling star,
This reed of sorrow standing by its stream.

Not now the wind, not now the water leaping
To ebb or flow, nor cricket left awake,
Nor any frightened word nor sound of weeping
Can turn you homeward from the path you take.
O hands untaught, that touched but could not break
The crystal box where ecstasy lay sleeping!

## IX—1960

If I should see you, if you were the same,
With the face you had, and summer, and that hair,
I would not know you, would not know your name.
You might cross my field like water or like air,
Or spray blown inland from some tall wave's wing,
As once you did, when I was watching where
Your footprints vanished by the moss-grown spring.

Why, I might think, what person walks this way
Along this path, leaving one footprint more?
Someone I knew, perhaps, another day?
Not you, but Time, went out and shut the door.
I would not wonder long, nor mark the spot,
Seeing you there unchanged, as I am not.

## Songs and Sonnets for a German Bartender—1938

### I

### Sonnet for Sunday Morning

Put by, put by that little glass of gin,
Nor think to hold its frail, pursuing spell.
Lulled by the sound of flute and violin,
Susie is sleeping sweetly where she fell.
Oh, stay no more while Morris breaks his neck,
And Horace hangs his trousers on the drum.
Call in the waiter, let him bring the check,
And come away, my beautiful and numb.

Oh, my beloved Herman, day repeats
Itself once more in lavender and onyx,
And milk is being carried through the streets
But once again in Brooklyn and the Bronyx.
Daylight has dawned again for me and you.
Come to the morgue and order slabs for two.

### II

Herman, you are not one whose dish
Dips lightly into passion's pond.
Your eye can be as cold as fish,
Whereby is quelled the ogling blonde.

The lads and lasses gone in drink,
The tipsy bottles stir you not;

Amid this coil of clack and clink,
You are, at times, a sobering thought.

At times, I see your heart as waiting
Emergencies that may arise,
As in a bowl behind a grating
A noble prairie oyster lies.

But oh, I love your whiskered pan,
That bearded headland through the haze,
You are a figure of a man
Would turn a gal to better ways.

By misted glass and foaming mug,
I see your curled mustachios sprout,
If you were ever in the jug,
I'd pay a lot to get you out.


### III

Whatever ailed our Susie no one knew.
It might have been her passion's unrequitals,
Or all unknown amongst our nightly chew
Some fox of gossip gnawed upon her vitals;
But suddenly she up and bit her fellow,
And said that Heinrich Heine was a Jew;
Turned round and kicked the fretwork off the cello,
At your cat, Herman, flung a dish of stew.

Oh, then behemoth clawed primeval clod!
I saw you, Herman, stiffen at your bar,
Come down across the carpet like a god
Who sees one of his mortals go too far.
You spanked her where it hurt and I approved.
It was a sight one could not see unmoved.

## IV

### Susie's Song

Some of you critters,
Some of you men,
I've got the jitters
Come again.

I wouldn't mention it,
I wouldn't crack,
But somebody's got to
Rub my back.

## V

### Song for New Year's Eve

Weltschmerz, my Herman,
Gesundheit.
What if the year
Passes out tonight,
Burns itself up
Like a ball of fluff
Flamed in a candle—
All *that* stuff?

The year's been nothing
To dance and shout
And carry on and
Brag about.

I've had notable
Lumps and knocks,
And you've had
Munich-on-the-rocks.

And no one supposes
It's coming up roses.

But tonight,
Gesundheit.
Let the damned chorus again
Squawk itself horus again.

I and my dress
And you and your tie,
Will give it a thing
To remember us by.

## VI

### Pavane for a Dead Hat

Over the mill,
Over the mill,
It hasn't come down,
So it's up there
Still.

Let it hang there,
Let it stay,
It wasn't becoming
Anyway.

## Pages from the History
## of a Sovereign State—1939

Parched and dry under the violent sun
Is the brown hill,
The grass dried to silver,
The dung of the horses to pebbles.
Under the live oak tree
Are small, sharp burrs,
Smelling of a curious kind of oil.
The live oak . . .
The relics of an old fence . . .
And the steep hill, up which the horses climb
Precariously.

The wind blows from the West,
From the Pacific,
Blows hard,
Bringing with it a homesick smell of weeds and water.
It melts the asphalt,
Burns the grapes,
Brings tears to the eyes of the real estate men.

The grass, silver as an old man's beard,
Scrattles like dry snow in the wind.
For months the land has been without rain.

But this valley,
Once an estuary of grass,
Part of an ocean of grass that stretched five hundred miles
From the Sierras through the San Joaquin . . .
This valley,

Which the Indians took from God,
Which the Dons took from the Indians,
Which the Pioneers took from the Dons
And sold to the Japanese and Italians in twenty-acre lots,
When the glutton roots of the fruit trees had lowered the
    water table,
And the codling moth had developed an immunity to arsenic,
This valley,
Black with thirst,
Lo!
Has hope again.

For the new four-lane concrete highway is finished,
Opening up the back country to the plain where the great
    coast cities lie.
They have driven a tunnel through the base of the solid
    mountain,
Four gray lanes, smooth as the flank of a Percheron mare.
And he who wants a country house in the real estate beyond
    the peaks,
No longer must drive steep hairpin turns on foggy nights.

Look up, Yaroshima Yoshimoto,
Los Angeles-born American citizen,
At the whisper of the white sidewall tires which stop outside
    your door.
Look up, Antonio Guerrierri,
From the tomatoes, which, jeeschris', the sun has blistered
    black.

Along the road where you hauled the drums of water
For the dying steers and the vines that bore no grapes
One year, and the next bore grapes that did not sell,
Come now the sons and grandsons of the Pioneers,
Following the wonderful, tireless machine
That digs the ditch for the municipal water company.

In the walnut grove where Pietro bled to death under his
    tractor,
Look at the sign, like a rising sun of hope:
CHOICE ACREAGE. CITY WATER. TWENTY MINUTES FROM
    TOWN.

There, next spring,
They will build their swimming pools.
(Not now, for the land is dry.
It's new and unspoiled country, ready for the buyers,
But don't try to sell it till the rains have made it green.)

Next spring,
The real estate agent,
Up to his knees in fresh green grass and flowers,
(Mustard and miner's lettuce,
And the wild morning-glory that the disc harrows could not
    kill)
Voice muted, as if he could scarcely bear the beauty,
The magnificence of this, God's land,
Will explain how the overflow from the pool can be used for
    the walnut trees,
Keep the grass glossy
And green.

The blood of the Indians did not do that,
Nor the blood of the Dons,
Nor Pietro's blood.
It takes the city water.

Oh, from May to November,
The land is parched and dry,
The grass silver as an old man's beard,
The horsedung scorched to hard, black stones;
But lovely country;
God's country now,

Twenty minutes from town by the new highway,
Now that the water is coming through,
Now that the water . . .

## 1940

Here it is, here it is again,
Gentlemen,
Cloaked in large phrases as it was before.
No knights in armor, this time, no military bands.
These soldiers weren't born then; they don't remember
    "Tipperary."

We were born then; we remember the glow
Of the young blood bustling, the high school parade,
The bayonets' glitter up front, the
Pride.

When the world was made safe for Democracy, the sailors
    of the Ward Line
Struck, and in Little Italy the first generation Italians
Wouldn't assimilate; they wouldn't even learn English.
What can you do with people like that?
A man and his wife and four children starved to death in the
    Yangtze Valley,
And a railroad dick kicked a couple of bums off a freight
    car between Pittsburgh and Chicago.

When we grow too old to dream, as we did in the popular song,
We'll remember the days when people began to get tired of
    being pushed around,
And the day before that, when the great man said,
"They hired the money, didn't they?"

## Overheard in a Bar—1940

No, I hope
The first bomb don't get me.
I want to be alive a while
To see what happens.
But with my luck
The first bomb will probably fall
Clunk on top of my dome.

That bakery in Manhattan—
I've forgotten the name of it,
I worked there once.
That was in thirty-two and the boss of it is dead now.
I didn't kill him, but I wish I had.
He was a bastard.

In nineteen-eighteen,
I was a kid in school,
And everybody said about what they're saying now.
I marched in all the parades,
I stood around and enjoyed it when some sailors tore the
    shirttail off an old Dutch cobbler,
And made him chew it up and swallow it.
I saw a fiery cross burning on the top of some hill or other—
    funny—I've forgotten where that was now.
And I thought that people were brave and strong and the men
    were tough and the women would fight like tigers,
If the Huns should happen to come off a U-boat
    and start cutting the children's hands off.
And so I would,

And so would you,
My fine-feathered friend.

Look.
In some year back along a time
I hated a man enough to kill him,
But I don't hate nobody now.
I don't feel nothing at all about this.
I got enough to eat, what with the business boom
And labor getting important again,
And hands needed on the machines.
Guys like me is worth more'n a dime a dozen now.

In the past ten years there was a time when I was hungry.
I ain't hungry now.
What I want's a car
And plenty of good roads to try it out on,
And a bush to lie under with my girl.

God's beer, I don't want to kill nobody now.

# The Barricades—1940

Listen.
We have chipped the stone,
We have carved the wood,
We have drawn the yellow maple leaf lying where it fell;
The land was beautiful to us,
And the gray clouds coming over the brown mountain
With the woodsmoke in the fall.

Listen.
There is a cave in the woods where an Indian once lived,
And in the clay, inside, the print of his narrow foot.
The panther has snuffled this footprint,
And the archaeologist;
The shaft of sunlight coming through the pine trees in the
     morning
Has lain upon it.
There is a secret in this cave.
The wind whispers it.
Listen.

Day-before-yesterday morning,
The day after the headlines in the papers,
We put down our mallet,
We laid our carving chisels carefully away in oil,
We ran our fingers over the smooth stone of the foundation,
And we said, "Rome was not built in a day."

No, it was not.
And Rome did not die in a day.

Rome died over a period of centuries with loud bellowings,
Like an old elephant in pain, that lives a while on whatever
    sick elephants live on.

Listen.
After this time,
During which Rome and the Indian cities have slept
    continuously in their brothers of graves,
On which we, in our lifetimes, have helped to heap the dust,
After this time, remind us to remember:
We carved the stone,
We chiseled the wood,
We worked delicately along the grain of walnut and pine,
And then, the day-after-yesterday morning,
We laid our tools away.

## Tuxedo Junction: or
## Where Was That Place?—1941

For a long time I was troubled by cities,
But not now;
And never anymore
Shall the dreams of men, tangible in steel and stone and
    mortar,
Trouble me when I am awake.

What do these do? I asked, leaning out of a window on
    Thirty-ninth Street,
What do these do, that hemlocks and pines or palm trees
    do not?
And why is the breath sucked from my lungs when I look
    at them?

Now I know why.
The names of the poets and painters and last year's best
    sellers
Are printed on the tablets and their likenesses put up in the
    halls of fame;
But who knows what man built this skyscraper?
Who was the architect? Did he have a wife, and was there
    a plaque upon his house,
Saying, *Here Mr. Blank lived and dreamed his dream?*
Or in any public park is there a concrete-mixer
    set upon a pedestal, with words saying:
*This was the tool he used, this was his machine?*

The public parks are reserved for the marble generals and
    their trusty horses—

Traveler, and the snow-white mount of General Washington.
There the infinite faces of foot-soldiers with rifles
Dream in stone above the cannon and the pyramid-piled
    cannon balls,
And the long lists of names saying who died and who came
    home;
Changed every twenty years for want of room.

When the blueprints are done with they are filed away and
    forgotten.
No one comes back to them and says, "This is a First Folio,"
    and draws his breath softly,
And goes away to remember the time he saw a First Folio.

Now I know why.
You read the headlines in the papers,
You listen to the radio,
And you tell me.

## Song to an Old Tune—1945

Oh, what did you get out of the war,
For you and no other?

All the things that we fought it for,
And there were a lot of them,
Brother.
A barrel, a bucket, a bag, a bin,
Space to put my possessions in,
A cedar chest and a carryall,
A house, a mansion, a tower, a hall,
A can, a closet, a cuspidor:
I got plenty out of the war.

And how did you find you could manage that,
For you and no other?

I used the headpiece under my hat,
And it's screwed on good,
Brother.
I put a flea in a fellow's ear,
I plucked a crow and a racketeer,
I made a guess and a couple of bets,
And I cornered a market in cigarettes.
I had ways, and an ear to the ground.
A man like me, he gets around.

And what will you do with all you've got
For you and no other?

I'll get off of the hot spot
Where I've always been,
Brother.
I learned my stuff in the times gone by,
When my kids was hungry and so was I;
So I got mine while the going was good,
And if I hadn't done it, someone else would.
It's me, now, with the trouser-crease,
I sat out the war and I'm in the grease,
And, Jesus willing, I'll live through the peace.

*Ecce signum, Brother.*

# Refugee—1945

She was an American civilian in Hong Kong
When the Japanese took the city;
She saw death,
Not decently, as we at home see death,
Embalmed in a coffin with carnations,
But splashed in shapeless masses on the stones of the street.

Now she is safe at home;
She lectures;
She has written a book.
She invariably ends her talk to the Women's Club
With "Why were we attacked? Why? Why?"

I have read her book.
In it she says, on page so-and-so,
"I had eight trunks,
Full of lovely things,
Picked up for a song from the dealers of the Far East . . .
Jade and jewelry,
Ivory,
Old scrolls,
A Buddha, carved a thousand years ago.
Matchless possessions that cost very little;
They were looted from me and I lost them."

On page such-and-such, again, she says,
(And listen, you ghosts of men who died at Hong Kong)
"Most of the roads are beautiful, fit for motor traffic,

But the steepest peak of the mountain, two thousand feet,
Is a matter for coolies and a sedan chair."

Why were we attacked? Why?

*Lady, for Christ's sweet sake,*
*Who do we think we are?*

## Advice to Mothers—1945

Mothers, take care what you do to your child
While he is wonderful and young.
Before you write upon him the terrible screed of your sorrows
Carve it upon a stone
Which may carry it forever to a grave in the secret earth
But cannot transmit it to its own son.

O mothers, look away from the magic mirror
Which holds you as the widow's arms the maiden!
Your child was not born a solace for your terror,
But for the world's, which he will find more laden
With fear than you, with more than your black sorrow,
If you do not look away from your own yesterday
Into his tomorrow.

Say to him, "Son, it is not a part of duty
To use this power I have over you for harm;
As a child, you have great dignity and beauty;
I see these—in your head upon my arm,
In your body's eagerness, in the love you have for me.
As best I can, I will teach you a man's manners,
But I will not destroy your beauty nor your dignity."

Say, "While you are with me, you shall not be lonely."
Say, many times, "I love you," and "My dear."
Say, "I am not quite the center of the universe; only
Know that whenever you need me, I am here."

O mothers, look around you at the marred children;
Look at the men of business, men of wars.
Look at the senators, Oh God, look at their faces
In the conference rooms where they wrangle over places
In the world's sun, with selfishness and noise.
Cut away sagging jowls, cut away scars
Of greed and insecurity and fright,
And what is left but the faces of little boys
Who cannot find their mothers in the night?

O mothers, send your son away from you
In armor, knowing love is in the world
(He will not understand this while he is little,
But he will remember it when he is grown!)
With the strong tendril of maturity curled
In his man's breast, and behind him no acid shame
From a dishonorable childhood.
Even then you will not be late for your bridge game;
Your homelife will still be nice;
And it may be that your son
Will not be one
Among the hearts of ice
Who paves
The world with graves.

## Lost Atlantis: A Threnody
## for Liberals—1965

There are no bells left to ring out under the water;
The ships that came are lost;
The sailors are all dead.
In the afternoon the eastwind blows fog through cellar
   windows.
The barns are burned. Woodbine grows in the shed
Where the nets hung once, smelling of brine and tar.

We, who were children then, how we are grown!
Our fingertips are of stone
And we are horny-hearted
From listening to spiders' conversations
All day long, while the winds of the world blow by.
We have come a great journey and now it is ending
Here in the flats and shallows of this land.
Were we the ones who with awe and wonder heard the sweet
   lonely ringing
Come up out of the water
Over the ledges and shingle
To the sand?

Like the warrior Greek, lost in his ancient maze,
We are lost in ourselves, fighting no foreign war.
We have come a voyage by many dangerous ways,
Setting a course neither by moon nor star.
For neither stars nor moon nor the charts available
Showed where to take a bearing for, nor how,
What harbors safe, what channels sailable.
Vega, The Crown, The Coffin, and The Plow,

Fools' fire at night across a trackless sea,
Grooved in their icy orbits; and so we,
Past the lost vigias and capes, stood in;
And thus we came into this roadstead Now.

And sleekly silken are the sails.
Let down the hook into the mud
Where neither time nor tide prevails.
The moulted hawks will sleep; they cry
No warning through the drowsy showers.
Whose spars are those against the sky?
Rest easy;
For they are not ours.

No.
We have come too far to travel now by lantern-light
Or in darkness, over roads not known to us.
Not now.

The gales howl in the passes, the beautiful brown bright river
    goes past its oxbow, secretly
Pointing to where our peace is, to where it hides in the wood.
We talk much about our peace, about finding it.
Let so much be said; if the saying so be good.

Peace is for those whose bloodstains are left upon them by
    battle, which ours are not.
Ours are the bruises of the bystander, not so innocent, on
    whom debris fell;
We are the casualties of the spent shot
From the battle of living in the world, and not
In an oh-so-private-and-personal hell.

I and my people make fine love; we grow
Grizzled behind our human faces; sound

Has power over us, and the earth's sweetness, but we know
We shall not be Noah, when the rest of the world is drowned.

Blow thistledown to the breeze, or the feather from the
    breast of the hawk,
But patch no sails.
Break out no bright new canvas to the gales
That drove us blind across the smoking sea
Laden with dreams below the Plimsoll-mark.

Our voyage has wrecked no vessel, found no grief,
Scattered no cargo on the sunny sand
For the polyp to make coral of, his reef
Our monument. We came to land
With courage on us like a lover's kiss,
And few of us even know that this
Is black as pitch upon the hoary ships,
Bitter as death upon a lover's lips.

Ring out, O bells, lost in the trackless water,
Echo, that long ago
Sweetened the foaming midnight, when our hulls
Reeled past the perilous headland
Drowned in snow.

Unheard, do we say? Yes.
For the doors of our ears are numb,
Deafened, beside our shallow sea,
By that clamor out of the waters
Thundering,
In derision, and
In mockery.

## The Man of Parts—1970

When time was up and his day began
The Indestructible Iron Man
Rose complete from his clockwork rest.
Humming sweetly, humming low,
The world's most intricate dynamo
Buzzed a tune in his mighty breast.

He was polished until he shone
Perfect down to his finest wheel.
Sanctified wire and holy steel
Made his arteries, nerves and bone.
Simple, unbreakable, easy to work,
Motion achieved by the flick of a lever,
First of his kind and all-out clever,
No blood to drip, no flesh to mortify,
Here was a sun to set men's watches by.

Now give your creature oil and let him go,
Whose meekness hath the earth inherited.
For him you labored, painfully and slow,
Winking the daylight in with eyes of lead.
See him beginning, how he sits and spits
His lovely sparks against your patch of stars.

He cannot know how pain untangles its
Inglorious coil, how folds above its scars.
He cannot die, nor see the leaves blow down
Over the weathered shingles of the town,
Nor hear the plover calling as it flies.

He is the Wonder shaped behind your eyes,
Out of the stockpile of the centuries
And the mind-midden of industrious dead;
Born of a spear, born of an arrowhead,
Crossbow and mace, grenade and Gatling gun,
And all his little wheels that sleekly run,
The track, the flange, the sealed and burnished ball,
Adapted from the creaking logs which once
Rolled up the siege machines to storm the wall.

Well done.
So let him go with tears and pride,
And cheer him on his way, and
Stand aside.

The thunderous west is ribbed with gold.
It is December. It is cold.
The winter moon comes rising gaunt and slow
To pluck at bare-boned beeches on the hill;
The frozen pond booms deeply and is still
Under its creaking rushes, banked with snow.
Slab-white the ice and bitter to the moon,
And delicate small frostflakes gather there;
And three old witches riding to the west,
Scale down like three dead leaves upon the air.

"Here's a place,
Under this bank."
"All right. Shove over,
You old crank."

"I want half and you two girls can each have a quarter."
"Why?"
"Because I'm the best witch."

"Well, get *her*, Victoria!

She's gone bats,
The crazy necromancer
Wants half the cats,
Half the lizards,
And half the mud,
And two full quarts
Of the dragon's blood.
And the rights to the moon
In the midnight sky!"
"So what about us?
When do we fly?"

"I don't care when you fly.
Just don't come into my part of it,
That's all."

"You heard her, Gladys.
Get out your bag.
We'll magic some sense
Into this old hag."

"Ssh-shush, Victoria!
Don't be a fool.
Think what she's got
In her reticule."

"Well, think what I carry
In the toe of my shoe.
A teaspoonful of it
Would pulverize you."

"Now, Evelyn.
Now, Evelyn.
Remember,
No witch is an island."

"I remember, all right.
No witch is an island
Who hadn't damn well better be."

*Oh, girls,*
*Don't argue.*
*Listen.*
*Please listen.*
*You hear the curled cold leaf crackle?*
*The boom in the iron pond?*
*The forest silence?*

"Look at my muscles!
Look at my hand!
I'm not water,
And I'm not sand . . ."

"Maybe you're not,
You ugly bitch,
But a plumber could make
A better witch."

"Is that so?
Buzz, buzz,
Bring on your magic,
See what it does!"

All night long till morning light
The voices cackle against the night;
The broomsticks shiver, the black cats cry,
On three warm hearthstones
The fires die.

Round the white pond with icy sound,
The stiff weeds chatter, stalk to stem,

Of what, awaking in the ground,
Must claim blood-brotherhood with them.
And the rising sun disperses gold
On three
Stalagmite
Pillars of cold.

We remember the sweets of summer, the salmon in the icy
    pool,
The plover crying up the milky dawn.
We remember no one immortal, wanting to live forever,
Only to find the patch of oxalis in the wood next year,
As last,
The tower of the maple
Green.

Large, bright machine,
Pillar of metal in the summer grass,
We are old and tired and wise.
We knew you when.
When you were chariot-wheels coming up the pass from
    Babylon;
When you were wild, half-broken horses galloping the streets
    of Rome.
We saw you in the cold, reptilian face
Looking out of the howdah on the war-elephant.

Bright pennon,
Brave glint of sun on spearpoints,
Camouflaged cannon,
Flowering of molecules lovelier than roses,
More orderly than the petals of chrysanthemums,
Our flesh and blood that was obsolete as long ago as when
    Nebuchadnezzar's bully-boys smashed down the hill towns,
Has met you, in your time, with shepherd's crooks,
Bare hands, Molotov cocktails, or plain stones.

You are what always goes the long way round to do the job
That any simple club would do as well.
Clank down the ages in your boots of steel!
We almost think
You must be good, you took so long to make.

## Tourist — 1971

He stopped his car beside my garden fence,
On a hot afternoon, the sun a pale disc, with fog coming in.
The Bermuda High was working north again
Against the cool air coming down from Canada.
We have this in June, in early July;
Sometimes all summer long.
Fog over the fabulous coast,
Often with rain.

In the tourist camps the beds are damp,
Outside, the fire will not burn.
Sometimes the wood is wet, or rotten.

He looked at me and said in a beaten voice,
"Where's the way to the Swan's Island Ferry?"

I said, "Go back to the general store, you've just passed it.
There's a sign. Follow the signs from it.
Take the dangerous corner past the sardine factory,
And on to the end of the road."

He drove off without a thank-you, but I had a look at his
    outfit;
A bone-tired wife, five children, the oldest fifteen or so,
Who complained, while he was talking, that *she* wasn't going to
    stay in any rotten place where there wasn't a swimming pool.

Watching him make his U-turn in my parking space,
I wondered about him.

Maybe he worked on an assembly-line somewhere; he had a
  look of it.
Automobiles? Atomic power plant? Oil refinery?
You couldn't say.

Now he was on the assembly-line of his vacation.
He had driven the turnpikes,
He had fed the family at Howard Johnson's,
He had seen the coast resort where the nineteenth-century
  great had lived and spent their money.
He had seen the lighthouse.
And now, quietly, he wanted to know where was the Swan's
  Island Ferry,
As if the turn by the general store
Might be the turn by Avernus to the ferry across the
  River Styx.

## Come All Ye Murderers, All—1971

Dead in the morning, the green tree
That held the eagle,
Comforted the wren;
The needled tower that rested tired eyes,
The home of mosses, sounding-board for woodpeckers,
Is down, cut down.
And all the king's men,
With bulldozers, hoists and cranes, loaders and trucks,
The things they have
To slice and move and dig
And load and push
And roll
And haul away,
Cannot put back one tree to grow upon its roots again.

## Short Poem for a Long Century—1971

Stupidity
Can ruin you,
Too.

## The Indian Shell Heap

In the bright light of morning the island lies still,
Around the shore the salt whisper of tide,
And over it, the sky.
Old thorn trees on the bank slant north and east,
Blown that way by generations of southwest wind.
Their leaves have a tough and northward-growing green,
And one has a thorn on which a shrike once pinned a sparrow.

Now, dried by seawinds, bleached by summer suns,
The delicate small bones hang loose, about to fall.
Let once the wind lean out a little more,
They'll blow away like straw, or the thorn will go.
The thorn is worn,
Sandpapered down to a thread by the slight-swinging bones of
    the sparrow.

This field was hayfield once.
This turf, ten inches thick, grew grass as high as a man,
From roots deep down in lime.
So they said.
Old Neighbor Welch's cows, they said, gave cream,
And his boys, fed on it, grew seven feet tall.
He plowed the turf up, once, and planted garden sass,
And had to haul the squashes home by ox-team, one at a
    time.

But that's all legend now.
The white man's town is gone from here, his houses down
Or open to the sky, his kitchen stove to rain.

In the barns that were fat and crammed and bulging,
Sweet-smelling to the peaks,
Swallows fly in and out where windows were;
Batten is gone from board and board from rafter,
Cracks here that a coon could walk through,
If there were any reason now for coons to come.
Old Neighbor and his sons sleep round the clock—
Who never, in the gone time, did such a thing, never,
When the foreshore field was full of hay to cut.

Dig in the foundations, lifting fallen rafters.
There you will find his tools.
Old iron—he was a one for saving iron.
Here, on an island, you couldn't run to a store,
Even if you had the cash to do it;
Couldn't run to a blacksmith shop when something cracked
    or wore,
You fixed it up yourself.
Old Neighbor made the things he used; could make a broadax,
An adze,
Horseshoes and horseshoe nails.

Dig here. The shelf in the barn where he kept the broadax
Has left its shape on the earth—
Rectangular, reddish, to show this soft stuff once was wood,
And ants live under it;
But here's the broadax where it dropped when the shelf fell
    down,
Under an old horse-collar and some rusty rings;
A pile of square-cut nails, what's left of the adze,
And two sickle-blades, plainly marked,
Each with the nickname of a seven-foot son;
Because the boys, Hiram and Byron,
Fought over whose tools were whose.
They had, it was said, some legendary fights,
Until the old man got enough of it.

He went to the barn, tore the iron shoe off an old wheel,
Beat out two blades at the forge, stamped one HI and one BY
And swore he'd use one on the nose of the first boy who
    yipped over tools from then on out.
These are the blades; you can still make out the letters:
HI and BY.


The hay in the field is only knee-high now.
It has had competition.
Thorn trees grow here,
The tough, spiked bush that loves a shell mound,
Pink wild roses, rattlebox on a fat root,
Daisy and devil's paintbrush—
Trash growth that in the gone time would have been whacked
    off by HI and BY,
Before their seeds grew big enough to know they were in a
    hayfield,
Growth known as "sour," whose roots nevertheless like lime,
For under ten inches of turf the shells lie heaped,
Clamshell and moon shell, winkle and scallop and snail,
Together with the bones of the great auk and the gray seal
    and the Indian dog,
Whose types died out of the world who knows how long ago.


Ten inches, at a hundred years an inch,
Of the slow-dying, slow-dropping grassroots cover them.
A thousand years of southwest winds and black northeasters,
Stars and sunrises, spring green and snow,
Since the Old Neighbor of his tribe split out his marrowbone,
Dropped his hammerstone by the firepit,
And went to sleep in the sun.


Slowly, carefully, dig, marking off the horizons
To the glacial clay, left when the ice went over.
Layer of ash, pearl gray, mixed with the black of charcoal,
Burned stones around the firepit which was his kitchen stove,

(And many years the rain's been dripping into it.)
Layer of beach gravel his boys lugged up from the shore
And dumped over the shells when they got high in the sun
And stank so a man couldn't sleep for the smell of them.
Shells, ash, charcoal,
And over all, a thousand years of turf.

Here by the firepit, you will find his tools,
Lost in the ashes, kicked aside by a careless foot,
Buried up, while the old man slept.
Did he beat up the boys, when he couldn't find this blade?
Give them sore tails and kick the kitchen pot?
At least, here is the blade in the ashes and the shards of
    the pot.

It is a knifeblade, carefully chipped from felsite,
Gray-green, tough stone, triangularly shaped.
The chips are tiny; the artist who split them off
Knew how to work the stone's conchoidal fracture so,
With nothing but a bone, or a beaver's tooth,
Or a chisel cut from antler.
(Not like a forge or a set of steel dies; without a micrometer.)
It must have taken whoever did it a long time.

Well, Old Neighbor, we have found it for you.
We'll put it on a shelf we have to keep,
Along with other artifacts we have,
HI's sickle and BY's sickle and a Dresden cup,
The sparrow's clean-bleached bones.
It may be we'll confuse the archaeologists
Who come to dig for keepsakes from a gone time
Under the red-brown rectangle of our shelf.
They'll think Old Neighbor had a Dresden cup,
And HI and BY and I all cut our hair with sickles.